GUITAR
Prep Test

Tunes and Pieces by
Vincent Lindsey-Clark

This book belongs to:

....

Date of Prep Test:

....

Examiner's signature:

....

The Associated Board of the Royal Schools of Music

GUITAR PREP TEST

Dear guitar player

The first step on a journey is always exciting. Some preparation before you begin is a good plan and makes the journey much smoother and easier. Your Prep Test will make sure you have all you need as you start your own musical journey and your teacher will guide you safely towards good playing that will last a lifetime.

The Prep Test is designed to be taken when you have been playing for a few terms. Built into it are all the sorts of skills you will be developing at this stage, such as a sense of pitch and rhythm, controlled and even playing, accuracy and quality of sound or 'tone'. The test takes around ten minutes to cover the tunes, pieces and listening games. You will be performing to a very experienced musician who will be interested to hear all that you do well and will also make suggestions to help you with your future playing. The examiner will write his or her comments on your certificate, which will be given to you at the end of the test.

We hope you enjoy the tunes, pieces and listening games, as well as the illustrations and Fun Page. We also hope that this is the first step of what will be an exciting and lifelong musical journey.

Now on to the music!

Clara Taylor

Chief Examiner

© 2001 by The Associated Board of the Royal Schools of Music   AB 2800

1 Tunes

The examiner will want to hear you play all three of these tunes. You will have to play them from memory, so once you have learnt them don't forget to keep your book closed when you are practising!

a) Two at a Time

Remember to play with right-hand fingers Rest Stroke and thumb Free Stroke. Aim for a strong melody line, and try to bring out the dynamics.

b) Chocolate Spread

There are different left-hand chord shapes in this tune. You will need to play these as block chords (striking the notes at the same time) or as arpeggios (playing the notes one after the other). Use Free Strokes throughout.

c) Tom Thumb

Practising this tune will help you to remember some useful bass notes. These are tricky to play if you do not have a good left-hand position, so try to bring your thumb down behind the neck of the guitar and keep your wrist out.

2 Set Piece

Your set piece can be any one of the five pieces printed on pages 6, 7, 8 and 9 – 'Balloon Race', 'Sad Clown', 'Soft Rain', 'Ball Game' or 'Spanish Dancer'. Your teacher will help you to choose the right piece.

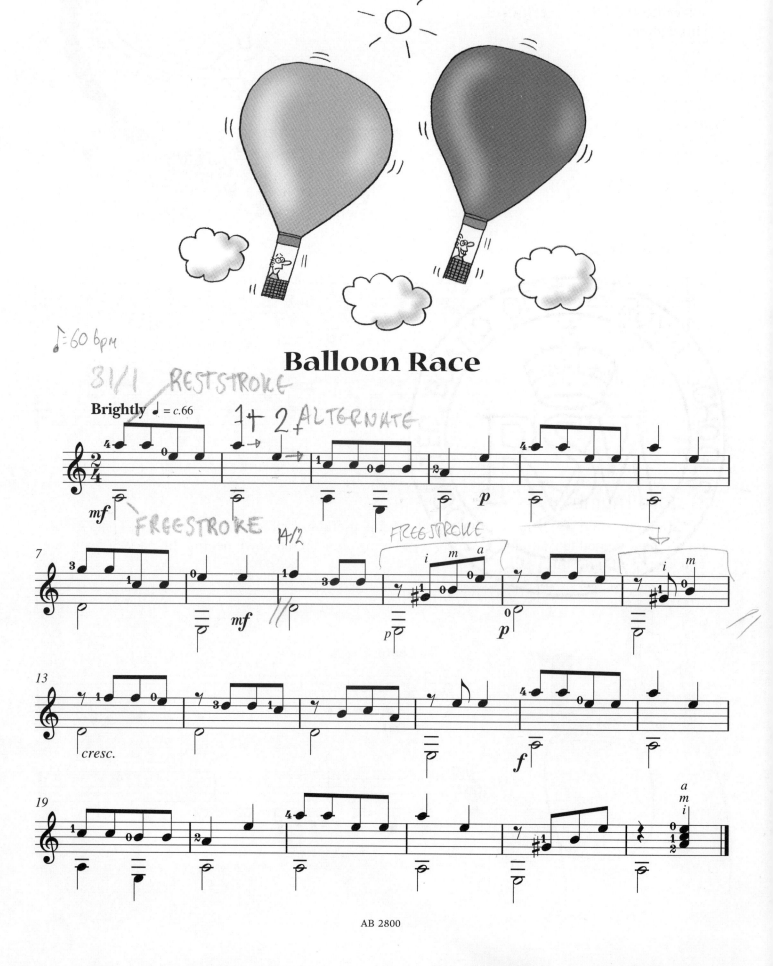

Balloon Race

Sad Clown

Soft Rain

Ball Game

Spanish Dancer

3 Own Choice Piece

This is the second piece you play and, because we want it to be something you really enjoy, we have left the choice of piece up to you. This means that you are free to choose any piece at all, even one of the set pieces from this book, as long as it is different from your first piece! Whichever piece you choose, don't forget to show it to the examiner who will want to know what you are going to play.

Your own choice piece can have a guitar or piano accompaniment, which can be played either by another guitarist or by the examiner on the piano. If you want the examiner to play with you, don't forget to bring a copy of the accompaniment.

4 Listening Games

In these games the examiner will be playing pieces of music like the examples printed below.

Game A: Clapping the beat

In this first game, the examiner will play a short piece in 2 or 3 time. You should join in as soon as possible by clapping or tapping the beat.

All music has a beat, so you can practise this game at home with your friends whenever you are listening to music on the radio or a recording.

Game B: Echoes

In this game, the examiner will clap two simple two-bar rhythms in 2 or 3 time. After each one, you should clap the rhythm back to the examiner in time and as an echo. The examiner will count in two bars before the first rhythm.

Practise this game at home with a friend or parent. Did you clap *exactly* the same rhythm? Did you clap it back in rhythm or was there a pause?

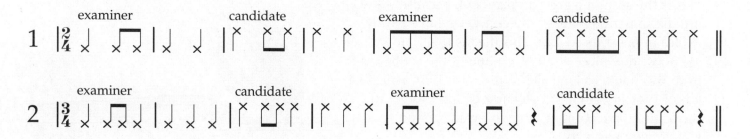

Game C: Finding the notes

Now the examiner will play a group of three notes to you, two times through. The game is to sing these notes back to the examiner after the second playing. They will be played in 'free time', so you don't need to worry about the rhythm. If you don't want to sing, you can play the notes on the first string of your guitar, in which case the examiner will play a group using only E, F and G – you have to find all three notes, including the starting note!

Game D: What can you hear?

In this last game, listen as the examiner plays another short piece of music. The examiner will want to know whether the piece was played loudly or quietly (the 'dynamic' of the piece), or whether it was fast or slow (the 'tempo' of the piece). The examiner will choose one of these and, before playing, will tell you which one to listen out for.

Practise this game at home with your friends whenever you are playing or listening to a piece of music.

Is this piece loud or quiet?

Haydn

Is this piece fast or slow?

Franck (adapted)

Fun Page

Music is written down on five lines known as a 'stave'. A few empty staves are printed below: you can use these to practise drawing notes, rests, clefs and time signatures (if you don't understand any of these words, ask your teacher or look in *First Steps in Music Theory* published by the Associated Board). Or you can write down some tunes of your own.

Word Search

This word search contains twelve musical words, listed below, which have been mentioned elsewhere in this book. How many can you find? Do you know what they all mean?

Words to find:
guitar
string
melody
note
chord
rhythm
dynamic
tempo
tone
arpeggio
stave
clef

B	R	H	Y	T	H	M	C	Q	S
E	O	S	B	W	O	I	H	A	T
P	M	I	R	C	M	T	O	N	E
A	E	G	Z	A	E	O	R	I	M
S	L	U	N	R	T	N	D	T	P
T	O	Y	E	O	B	I	G	R	O
R	D	H	C	S	T	F	U	N	H
I	Y	K	O	L	N	E	X	G	M
N	J	A	R	P	E	G	G	I	O
G	E	V	A	T	S	F	Y	A	V

We hope you enjoyed doing the Prep Test and look forward to seeing you at Grade 1!

10.01   Printed in England by Caligraving Limited, Thetford, Norfolk